NOT
GOD

NOT
GOD

A Play in Verse

MARC J. STRAUS

TriQuarterly Books
Northwestern University Press
Evanston, Illinois

TriQuarterly Books
Northwestern University Press
www.nupress.northwestern.edu

Printed in the United States of America

10 9 8 7 6 5 4 3 2 1

ISBN 0-8101-5168-5 (cloth)
ISBN 0-8101-5169-3 (paper)

Grateful acknowledgment is made to the journals where these poems first appeared, some
in slightly different form: *American Journal of Medicine* ("Bittersweet," "Brine," "Cancer
Prayer," "Eleventh Floor," "Mr. Biggers," "Semaphore"); *Black Warrior Review* ("Luck");
The Bridge ("Two Weeks"); *European Judaism* ("Chimes"); *Fan Magazine* ("Shoe Box");
Hadassah Magazine ("Chapel"); *Jewish Currents* ("Doldrums"); *Journal of Medical Humanities*
("Four Weeks," "Humming," "Names," "Paper Cups," "Sign!"); *Kenyon Review* ("Lecture
to Third-Year Medical Students"); *Minnesota Review* ("Apocalyptic Prayer," "Guide Wire");
Mudfish ("Sand Crab"); *Passager* ("Grandma Katy" [as "On the 25th Year of My Grand-
mother's Death"]); *Ploughshares* ("Alchemy," "One Word," "Sigh"); *Poetry East* ("Not God,"
"Say Yes"); *Prairie Schooner* ("Wound"); *River Styx* ("Apple Cores"); *Snail's Pace* ("The Size
of the Lesion"); *Spoon River Poetry Review* ("What'd I Say"); *TriQuarterly* ("What I Am");
and *Virginia Quarterly Review* ("Like Me").

Several of these poems were previously published in *Symmetry* (Evanston, Ill.: TriQuar-
terly Books/Northwestern University Press, 2000) or *One Word* (Evanston, Ill.: TriQuarterly
Books/Northwestern University Press, 1994).

Library of Congress Cataloging-in-Publication data are available from the Library of
Congress.

♾ The paper used in this publication meets the minimum requirements of the American
National Standard for Information Sciences—Permanence of Paper for Printed Library
Materials, ANSI z39.48-1992.

For Stephen Ezra Straus, M.D.,
my younger brother

CONTENTS

An early version of *Not God,* entitled *The Bridge* and consisting of twenty-five monologues in the voice of a patient, had its premier stage performance at the State University of New York, Theater Arts Program, in Purchase, New York, on April 13, 2000. It was directed and produced by Larry Kornfield, with Jacqueline Brogan as the patient. The play was subsequently performed at Franklin and Marshall College in Lancaster, Pennsylvania, on February 6, 2001; at the Lancaster Country Day School on September 17, 2002; and at the Bayer Institute Conference in Pacific Grove, California, on September 23, 2002. The first two performances were directed by Dorothy Louise, and Laura Howell played the patient in all three.

Not God had its premier stage production at the York Theatre Company in New York City on April 21, 2004. It was produced and staged by Louis Chiodo and directed by Vincent Scarpinato, with music composition by Patrick Barnes. Tom Bozell played the doctor, and Mary Kay Adams played the patient. The play was subsequently performed at Baruch College's Engelman Recital Hall (artistic directors Robert LuPone and Bernard Telsey) in New York City on November 12, 2004. It was produced by MCC Theater and directed by Lisa Peterson, with Stephen Willems as literary director and William Cantler as casting director. David Chandler played the doctor, and Becky Ann Baker the patient.

The Bridge: A Journey Through Illness, a museum multimedia exhibition, was at Lehigh University's Zoellner Arts Center in Bethlehem, Pennsylvania, from April 7 to June 20, 2004. The exhibit, featuring artwork by Rick Levinson, was curated by Ricardo Viera. Lehigh University published the exhibition catalog with essays by John Yau. The photographs by Theo Anderson within this book are from *The Bridge.*

A NOTE FROM THE PLAYWRIGHT

Not God, a play in two acts, consists of individual poems presented as monologues by a patient and a doctor. In the opening monologue, the audience discovers that for two weeks the patient has been in the hospital, a foreign and forbidding place for most but one where it's possible to become an insider, learning to translate sounds and nuances. The audience knows only what the patient chooses to tell, much of which is based on whatever is happening to the patient at the moment: a test, visitors, news about results, treatment. The doctor, too, reacts to items of the moment—patient results, dysfunctional hospital systems—as well as to reminiscences of life outside the hospital. It is assumed that this is the patient's physician, but little in the play suggests that they ever address each other directly. They have one common concern, the health of the patient; beyond that, their stories are divergent.

Gender is not specified for either character, and a character may change gender one or more times throughout the play. Nonetheless, certain patient monologues (such as "Names") are better suited to a woman, while other doctor monologues (such as "Shoe Box" and "Not God") work best with a man. The patient may assume different personae (in one production, the patient began and ended as a middle-aged suburban sophisticate but in between was an elderly African American woman, a Jewish New Yorker, and others), and the patient and doctor may switch roles during the performance. The play does not lend itself to a highly stylized or elaborate set. A spare stage set is preferred, with limited, if any, props: a hospital bed, a chair, a desk, an IV pole. Costumes, too, are simple: a dress or hospital gown, a lab coat. (To suggest baldness—and the illness's severity—the patient in one production wore a head covering, which was removed early in the patient's final speech.) The actors may move around the stage or simply stand or sit midstage for the duration of the play. A contemporary score for cello was composed for one production, though others did not use music. Actors may hum between such monologues as "Humming" and "Chimes," and ambient sound has included clicks and beeps of hospital machines.

This edition includes a few scenes not performed heretofore. With the exception of the first monologue, "Two Weeks," and the patient's final monologue, "The Bridge 2," the order is somewhat open to change, though chronological integrity is required to track the duration of hospitalization and the clinical path of the patient. Similarly, some monologues of the doctor clearly follow a certain order. Consecutive monologues may be merged, with actors alternating segments (for example, "Angiogenesis Factor" with "Lilies of the Field," and "Bittersweet" with "The Natatorium"). Titles are generally not spoken, though exceptions might be made for such pieces as "Two Weeks," "Lecture to Third-Year Medical Students," and "Four Weeks."

Because of these invited latitudes, how *Not God* is staged is open to interpretation. For that reason, staging directions are not included in the play.

NOT
GOD

CHARACTERS

Patient

Doctor

ACT
ONE

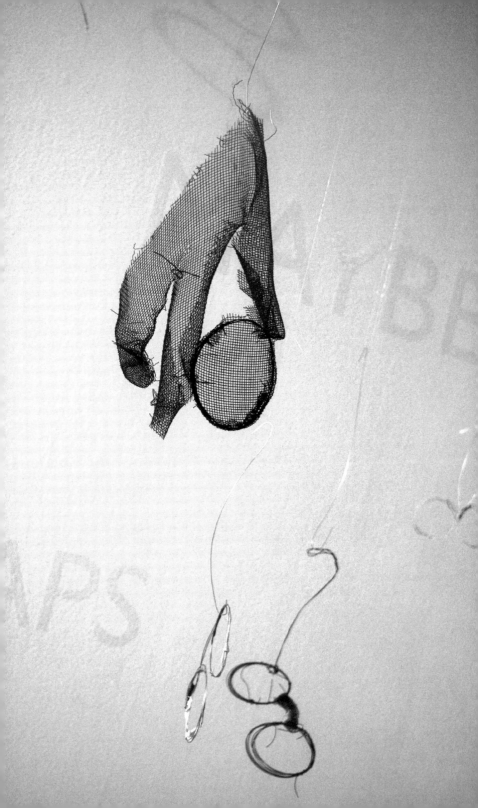

TWO WEEKS

Patient:

A man's cough bounces down the hallway
like pick-up sticks. Three rooms away
an IV machine beeps constantly. I know
the distance by now. I know Mrs. Applebaum
was discharged today and Mr. Singer
died. Not just the overhead intercom blaring
Code Blue or everyone running to his door.
It was the stillness afterward, the leaden walk
of the nurses. They've seen it before, but death fills
their shoes. They pass the pills in silence
and at the station their conversation is muted.
I asked Angela. She said he was old and frail
and his kidneys failed.
It is more than
she should say, but she is kind
to differentiate his circumstance from mine.
I am here now two weeks.

SAND CRAB

Doctor:

I recently walked along the bay
with my five-year-old nephew.
What are those little holes
with bubbles coming out?
he asked. Sand crabs, I said.
They hide under a thin layer
of sand to protect themselves.

Have you ever seen one?
he wanted to know. Yes,
I said, thinking of my first day
at the Washington V.A. hospital.
A young man, age twenty-two,
was hidden under a white sheet.
He was pale as a moonbeam,

and his mouth puckered
in and out with each breath.
He returned from Vietnam
with acute leukemia. His name
was Howard, I said
out loud. You're making
it up, my nephew laughed.

MR. BIGGERS

Patient:

I have a friend, Jeannie Mayer, who says that
a name tells us a lot about the person, much the same way
that dog owners often bear a resemblance to their dogs.
While I've given little credence heretofore to this homespun
philosophy (Jeannie isn't exactly Kant or Descartes), lately
I see its wisdom. Dr. Plummer is a urologist on staff. Then, too,
there is Mrs. Muffin, a nurse's aide who gives out breakfast.
Nurse Nancy Smith behaves quite anonymously, and
Joan Desirée, R.N., is the local heartthrob with whom
Dr. Robert Radcliffe is cheating on his wife. These are things
you come to know. Secrets waft out through porous walls.
I am in the midst of an oceanic all-day soap opera, I say to
Mr. Biggers, who nods as he mops vigorously under my bed.

ONE WORD

Doctor:

A man at the bus stop stooped
to retrieve a dime rolling toward
the drain. Looking at me, he said,
No ordinary dime, mister. Really? I said,

thinking how life is sometimes reduced
to a single word, a reflex, a courtesy.
Like the time I interviewed this young man
for a job in my lab, my mind wandering,

not attached to the conversation,
at best noticing his outdated tie.
Perhaps in response to some statement,
I said, Why? Then sensing the opportunity

he answered more eloquently, and that changed
everything. Like the time a woman walked
into my medical office for one thing,
and I put my fingers in the crevice of her neck,

the right side, and touched a fullness
deep within, and I knew that moment
I would say one word to her and nothing
would ever be the same again.

ANYWAY

Patient:

A week before I was admitted here
I was in the Metropolitan Museum. I was obliged
to go—you know, a fund-raiser
for the local arts council. I've been active
for years. They support amateur theater
at the library. I once thought of playwriting,
but I have no talent. Anyway,
there was a painting by Pontormo
that was transfixing. I've never responded like that
before—not to Rembrandt, Titian, or even
van Gogh. He was a solitary boy with one eye
shifted slightly. Strabismus, right?
Anyway, he was so sad, about thirteen,
dressed in blue velvet and lace. Something
troubled him deeply, and he was trying
so hard to be grown up, as if too much
was expected of him. Anyway, I was still nauseated
from my chemo this morning and I was thinking
about that painting . . .

THE SIZE OF THE LESION

Doctor:

Almost time now, a patient said. For what?
I wondered, knowing I wouldn't ask,
some things better left unsaid, leaving
the possibility of a different

interpretation. It's this way more
as time goes on. A daughter comes in late
and you don't say exactly what you feel
and her vague answer is probably

all you want to hear. Patients are proficient
at this. You tell them the X-ray showed
little change, knowing they won't ask
if the lesion's a little smaller or larger.

ROCKY ROAD

Patient:

I suddenly have a craving for Chinese oolong tea.
For Mrs. Sudbury down the hall it is ice cream.
This I relate to easily. When my mother was ill
and lost forty pounds (though still not skinny by any means),
she was admonished to take in more nourishment.
All her life she craved ice cream, but now a cholesterol of 350
was forgiven. The creamier the better. Cherry Garcia,
Chocolate Marshmallow Swirl, Oreo Cookie Crunch—
just the names brought her rapture. Dr. Donovan says
I can have strawberry milk shakes for breakfast.
Forget lamb chops. They taste like tires. Bring me
a large bowl of Rocky Road topped with Reese's Pieces
and a midnight snack of Double Rich Black Forest Seven-Layer Cake
with lots of almonds. Oh, it is almost worth being sick
if we can indulge that thing we most crave
without guilt: delicious, foolish, and obscenely rich.

SCARLET CROWN

Doctor:

I met a man my age running a greenhouse.
He pointed to the pots with pride, saying
they contained a thousand separate cacti.
Not much interest in these when I started,
he said. He pointed to the barbed bristles

(glochids), the bearing cushions (areoles),
and the names of many of the two hundred genera:
brain, button, cow tongue, hot dog, lace,
coral, and *silver ball.* In my work,
I said, I'm burdened with such straight-

forward terms: *lung cancer, lymphoma,*
breast cancer, leukemia. I'd love
to switch to *pond lily, star,*
or *scarlet crown.* Really? he said,
pointing to other plants named

hatchet, devil, dagger, hook, and
snake. Or perhaps a diagnosis of this:
rattail, white chin, wooly torch,
or *dancing bones.*

PAPER CUPS

Patient:

Charlotte awakens me at daybreak
to pass out pills from little paper cups.
There must be at least five medications
per patient, I tell her after quick computation.
More, she answers. The unit isn't filled
today. So how do you keep track
with all those paper cups? I want to know.
I tear off a small piece of cardboard, she says,
write your names, and place it underneath.
Isn't there a possibility for mistake?
Oh no, she answers. The greens
are placebos. They do no harm. This yellow one,
shaped like an octagon, is for heartburn.
Who couldn't use that? And the pink one—
you're the only one on it. I hope
you're joking, I say. Of course not,
she says, shaking out two blue oblongs
and handing one to me.

PINE NUTS

Doctor:

Just five pine nuts and my nausea
from the Platinol is gone, a thirty-two-
year-old woman in the chemo room told me
today. A man undergoing similar treatment nearby
offered that wrapping one's face in a hot towel

soaked in mentholated oil works much better.
By now I have heard countless anecdotal remedies
that are probably ineffective except for
their placebo effect. Yet each time I think to
dissuade their use, I have to remind myself

of an incident when I was five. I had fractured
my right forearm against our stoop,
having attempted to ride down its six cement steps
on my new twenty-inch Schwinn. Grandma Katy
washed and then wrapped my badly discolored

skin in a cool compress of honey, tree sap
(from a pine, I presume), and another ingredient
that smelled a lot like cesspool sediment. The pain
disappeared completely, and my bones were set
some three hours later without anesthesia.

ELEVENTH FLOOR

Patient:

A van near the west parking lot sells bagels,
jelly rolls, hot dogs, and soda. I can't read its sign
from here, but I see a workman holding a can
in one hand and with the other eating food
from a paper wrapper. I don't know why
they design these buildings so high. A conference
on hospital architecture should have been convened
to establish the optimum height. I doubt many
have paid attention to this. What if
a patient is acrophobic? Wouldn't it be better
if they were level with a flowering dogwood,
a Japanese maple? From here I look down
on sunsets. Why the eleventh floor? Admissions
is on the first, radiology the second, surgery the third,
pediatrics the fourth, obstetrics the fifth. Everyone knows
what's in the basement. Perhaps that's why
oncology is so far away.

APOCALYPTIC PRAYER

Doctor:

The apocalyptic prayer Sister Mary mouthed
in the chemo room was a touch too loud
and had the sibilance of a dirge, but nonetheless
Thomas Borland chimed in with a slow hymn,
a southern spiritual, I guessed, and then Rabbi
Goldfine began a Hasidic chant, the kind
generally accompanied by clarinet, and elderly
Mrs. Booth . . .

You can imagine how this must have sounded,
a cacophony of five or six patients
all singing in different keys. But in fact
it was something akin to a choral symphony,
the voices discrete instruments precisely
timed together. Afterward Sister Mary said,
Please, everyone, try your best to be on time
next week.

DOLDRUMS

Patient:

They come to give cheer: nurses, candy stripers,
elderly volunteers . . . and Aunt Ethel. At age six
I secretly believed she was the Wicked Witch
of the West. Today she reminds me why as she bounds in
blowing a kiss and wearing black stockings, red miniskirt,
and faux mink stole (and this is summer). She has cornered
a man again, poor seventy-five-year-old Harold from Miami,
who believes she's far younger than eighty-three.
I listen to her litany of complaints, bone by bone,
as she devours all the candy she's brought. She fills me in
on the gossip, looks at her watch, and springs up.
Your old aunt was here to lift you out of the doldrums,
she waves, teetering out the door on three-inch heels.
I laugh so hard I have a coughing fit. The family
all mock this old painted bird. But just now
I love her dearly, so irreverent and beautiful.

ANGIOGENESIS FACTOR

Doctor:

How did this happen? they always
ask. Someday I'm going to say, It starts
as a mutation, a deletion at chromosome
19, inherited no doubt—that
tumor promoters, carcinogens, transform

the cells over twenty years. First
dysplastic, then neoplastic. That
angiogenesis factor augments metastasis
elsewhere, and . . . By now they look at me

limp-lipped numb. And that took
six years to learn, to assimilate,
I want to add, and all you want to hear
is—I don't know. No one knows
how this happens.

LILIES OF THE FIELD

Patient:

This basket of flowers is stunning
but I wish they'd stop sending them—
my room is a veritable botanical forest.
And the thing is, most wilt in two days,
and as for the rest—I don't have a predilection
for spending an hour a day maintaining them,
so I give several to Angela to pass out
to the staff. And what do they think
I can do with six hundred pounds of candy
and gargantuan fruit baskets? And why
in God's name must Aunt Bertha visit daily?
She is so dark and elephantine and showers me
with despondency.
I should have been
more protective of my father
in that last aching month.

APPLE CORES

Doctor:

Suppose, just suppose, you're shown
an apple core and asked to describe
its inside, having seen hundreds before
    (they've all been pretty much the same),
but the question put to you,
almost as a matter of life and death,
    makes you wary—there may be
an exception, a core unlike any you've ever seen,
yellow and luminescent with garnetlike seeds,
    or no seeds, or no core.
Do you generalize, not having analyzed
the issue, having no statistical data?

    And even if you knew everything
about apple cores, the very latest studies
and their methodology, would you answer
    simply, or would you equivocate,
knowing each word is a shard of glass,
translucent, dazzling, and dangerous?

CRICKET

They keep this place so clean. It's
Hector, a slight elderly Hispanic man
who mops here twice a day. Twice a week
he uses an industrial polisher. We barely
converse. Today I said, Hector,
I hear a cricket in this room. He was mortified
and began to search behind the radiator
and under the bed until I was able to explain
I was teasing. I apologized. I told him
how much I rely on him that this room is
meticulous. After three weeks in this hospital
it's almost the only thing I can count on.

23

SAY YES

Doctor:

If I cut down on fatty foods, lose
fifteen pounds, work out three times
a week, will I avoid a heart attack?

If only every question were that simple.
It's an opportunity to answer unequivocally,
to give patients a sense of purpose

and hope, even if they've always been obese,
refractory to treatment, unable to comply
with a regimen. Still, just to say yes

is palliative, even though they know
the answer isn't accurate. They don't want
to hear statistics and vacillation.

Just to be like the surgeon who says,
It's a hundred percent curable—I got it all, omitting
the possibility that a cell, a micro-

metastasis, may already be elsewhere.
Say yes—a sliver of grace in an
excoriated world. I must try it sometime.

HUMMING

Patient:

I find myself humming at odd intervals. Sarabeth
pokes her head in my room and looks quizzically
at me. What can I say? I am unaware
of it. Oh, a Handel oratorio, I volunteer.
Sounds a bit more like Madonna, she says, smiling.
Albert, the phlebotomy tech, advises I write it down.
Retro rap, he calls it. Mrs. Quinlin's little granddaughter,
Allison, visiting this morning, started tap dancing, and
Monsignor Brady, praying at the next bedside yesterday,
offered that it reminded him of a holy incantation he heard
as a seminary student in Perugia many years ago.
I am confounded by these inexplicable noises
from my mouth that each recognizes as familiar. I think
God hears them as my prayers.

CHIMES

Doctor:

It sounded like chimes. How else
would a five-year-old hear an anapestic
beat, Aramaic, with an internal rhyme?

Kaddish de-rabbanan, a prayer for the dead,
an incantation said on the Sabbath
and High Holidays. I knew it by heart,
this sonorous dirge—quick alliteration,
hard-voweled words, and in retrospect

the first poem I learned. I admit now
I liked it. Early on I was asked
to lead the congregation. I would liken
my voice to a violin, the bowstring

drawing out its three beats, attenuating
the first two, slowing, stretching the last
with vibrato. The women would cry. The old men
would wrap themselves tightly in their tallisim.

I did this regularly, and yet I never understood
the meaning. What was the point? All the prayers
seemed the same in English. God's power, God's
goodness, man's weakness. It was the sound

I loved, church bells on a Sunday morning
in Tuscany, Bloch's cello concerto, second
movement. Even when my father died
and I was required to say the Kaddish every day

for eleven months, I'd close my eyes.
I am five, listening to its chimes: *b'alma
di v'ra khir'utei, v'yamlikh malkhutei.*

MRI

Patient:

This is the fifth time I am inside this narrow MRI
that abounds with metaphor. (At least I'm not
claustrophobic.) Dr. Johannson will scan it on his console
and ask Larry to go back and take smaller field cuts.
As they wheel me out I ask to know the results.
You have to wait for your doctor, Arnie answers. I tell him
that I know they've already seen it, that my doctor
won't be in until the morning, that there is no sense
keeping me in suspense, that my brother-in-law
is a doctor on staff (the only lie). This conversation
is repeated verbatim each time. Of course
they won't tell me. But by now I know it's not
simply because it's bad news.

SEMAPHORE

Doctor:

Sometimes a word seems to fall
into an inaccessible gyrus
     of my brain and is lost forever.

Then there are times it snaps back,
coursing up from a hidden sulcus,
     bounding across thousands

of synapses. *Adamantine* recently
did that. It was a word I once read
     and never looked up.

Then this week—*brindled, gibbous,
Rift Valley fever, Gaucher's disease.*
     In medical school I depended on

my excellent memory. I was quick.
I gathered them in, each word
     a shibboleth to be placed

in its proper quarry. Again today
a patient I often see was in and
     I couldn't remember her name,

but then a girlfriend's phone number
from tenth grade came to mind.
      That's the proof. It's all there

carefully tucked away. Everything
is recoverable: *agnosia, semaphore,*
      von Hippel-Lindau disease.

THE RED HERRING

Patient:

See this headline: A RED HERRING WASHED UP THURSDAY
NEAR THE BRONX RIVER PARKWAY. The reporter quoted
the Department of Fisheries: "No red herring
has been documented in the U.S. this century. . . .

We're checking the river for other herrings" and
"At NYU, a graduate student is writing her thesis
on the finding with a major symposium
scheduled for April." Does anyone really believe

such stuff? Someone undoubtedly
bought a fresh red herring that morning
at Hunts Point Market and it fell
out of the bag near Hartsdale.

BITTERSWEET

Patient:

Tapioca, cranberry yogurt, apple corn fritters.
Some things come conflicted—but you acquire
a taste for them. This is what I've learned lying
in this hospital bed three weeks. Take a test—
the IV hurts a little. Wait for the results—they are
ambiguous. Maybe do the test again. And the thing is,
my doctors all speak without definition. If I could,
I would ordain that *might, maybe,* and *perhaps* be expunged.
At least the Irish priest visiting my neighbor
was definitive. He said heaven is an eternal gift.

Everything here is bittersweet, spooned out
in dollops of castor oil with a little saccharin mixed in.

THE NATATORIUM

Doctor:

Natatorium, a nicer name for a pool, though
balneary sounds better. *Blemish, blotch, blister,*
spot have a practical imprecision, unlike *blackhead,*

wart, or *T cell lymphoma.* In this business
of oncology we prefer gray-faced
vertiginous words that quiver along a fault line.

Take *ascites,* for instance: the abdomen
is distended with liters of fluid. We say
excess water and *swelling of the belly,* knowing

full well that in this middle-aged woman
with no evidence of liver disease,
an ovarian cancer is almost certain.

LUCK

Patient:

Here's a good one I saw
on an obscure cable station today.

(I think they mostly interview farmers who see aliens
land in their cornfields and housewives

inhabiting someone else's body.) So this middle-aged
man was saying how he gave up smoking last month

and now his surgeon just told him there's a lesion
in his lung and it's lucky because it's curable.

So this man (I think from Pittsburgh) says, Just like
it's lucky for those two kids pulled from

a burning building. If it's lucky, how come
they got second-degree burns? How come

they were in the building in the first place? Want to hear
about real luck? he says, staring straight at the camera.

I have this itch under my arm. I'll scratch it twice
in slow circles and my cancer is gone.

SHOE BOX

Doctor:

Sooner or later it returns to
    my cards fastidiously kept
age five to fifteen   five-cent packs
    with flat pink bubble gum,
won with dexterity   two and a half flips
    from the hip   a leaner   a used
Mickey Mantle for Mel Ott
    a mint Honus Wagner today
worth $600,000   thrown away
    discarded by my mother
when we moved to Ocean Parkway
    apartment 6F with a terrace
rear room facing the alley   because
    a man offered my father $46,000
for our house   a size 8½ double E
    shoe box   2,000 cards cataloged
ten years   and now I tell my wife my
    two children my dog my poet
friend who plays left field my
    analyst   that my childhood
vanished in that box.

THE BRIDGE 1

Patient:

A fascinating article in today's science section:
a suspension bridge near Bucharest built in the 1890s
with two terminal towers and ultrathin cables
has never needed repair. Spectrographic analysis suggests
that the cable's seven twisted strands are made of an alloy
much like titanium, and, more remarkable,

its high central tower, which engineers have argued for years
should have led to critical instability of the bridge,
has easily withstood hurricanes and even bombardment
by both the Nazis and Russians. The original drawings
are lost, but recent, though incomplete, thermal mapping
of its pillars identified a unique pulley system.

They now speculate that these titaniumlike cables,
pulleys, and middle tower provide an almost limitless
weight-bearing capacity.

I was never good at volleyball. I can't
sail. I've never been to Bangkok or Peru.
I've published twenty-two papers on early
adolescence. Mostly theoretical. Like measuring
intellect. Like imagining a bridge that can cross
the Atlantic. Like imagining sound
without my children.

My daddy whispers algebraic equations
to me, ancient paradigms, he says,
taught to him in heaven by Copernicus.
What is its purpose? I ask. To understand
monumentality, he responds.
The bridge has seven layers of titanium
le bound together by intention

ted in recitations. Seventeen
n safeguard the structure.
ates in the middle tower while
enth sings lullabies.

I am confounded by these inexplicable noises
from my mouth each recognizes as familiar. I think
God hears them as my prayers.

SIGH

Patient:

I sighed this morning, a slow deep inspiration
that dragged the air into the recesses of my lungs,
portions I imagine had been forgotten
in the last few months. And then for a second
or two I felt the life pass out of me.
As if it were a prelude, a taste for the sake
of recognition, to diminish my anger.
As if it were a gift to make me more accepting,
so that when the angel lifts my hand
onto her atomless sleeve I will have no animosity.
She is so like my physician. He has no tolerance
for remonstration, his head is so cluttered
with obligatory data. I might articulate my pain
but he is filled with dying and I'm obliged
to keep the sigh inside.

MONDAY

Doctor:

Monday in Miami Beach. Everyone is eighty-two. Fourteen men
walking on the boardwalk look exactly like my father.

It is inauguration day in Washington, Martin Luther King
Day, and back in New York the temperature's

twenty-two. The last time I was here I spent three days
in the I.C.U., my father on a cardiac monitor, IVs

supporting his pressure. I am attending a conference
on memory. An anthropologist spoke about anti-

aesthetics in the museum world. A curator talked about
the controversy surrounding the installation of the cattle car

in the Holocaust Museum, how a survivor on the board
refused to step into the building if she was required

to walk through. I am thinking about Mr. Vallone.
The pain in his hip has increased again and the P.S.A.

levels are higher. I am thinking about my father returning
three months later jaundiced, about his sister who said

I was criminal to treat him, about the day he had gram-negative
sepsis, the walk we took in Belle Harbor after

he responded. A man going by has the same mustache.
My father asked me to grow a beard. I kept it six years

after he died, and then it was gray, and my son married.
I am trying to think of a treatment for Mr. Vallone.

N.P.O.

Patient:

Angela passes out pills from little cups. It is all
so archaic, I think, waiting outside the CAT scan room
on a cold rubber cot covered with a thin cotton blanket.
My behind will show if I stand because the gown can't close
in the back. Why is that? I asked Nancy yesterday,
never expecting an answer. She said it was in case
of emergency; to remove them quickly.
It's one P.M. The CAT scan is delayed again
and I haven't eaten since midnight. Can you get me some lunch?
I say to a tech walking by. He points to the sticker. You are N.P.O.,
he says. But the CAT scan is put off, I explain, and by the time
they get me upstairs lunch will be over. Let me see
what I can do, he nods, walking away. I have a mind
to grab my chart, the blue plastic binder at the foot of the bed.
I have a mind to rip off that sticker.

BLUE STONE

Doctor:

At ten A.M. the MRI went down, I can't
retrieve a C.B.C., and the nephrologist's note
is illegible. Every day systems fail,
procedures delay. I am thinking that
the hospital is like some mortal being
transmogrified by unseen gremlins.

They are in the X-ray machines, the
phone system, the coffee cups. They
even make pencils break. In this business
of illness you never know when something
will go wrong, when a round blue stone
will fall from heaven and shatter your bone.

CHAPEL

Patient:

There is a chapel downstairs. I passed it twice
on the way to radiology. No one was inside.
There are twelve wooden benches, a large crucifix,
and stained glass above the altar. A note in the elevator says
RELIGIOUS SERVICES FOR JEWS AVAILABLE ON REQUEST.
Today a priest came in and offered me absolution.
I think you have the wrong room, Father,
I said. He checked his notes, laughed courteously, and replied,
Now that I'm here . . . A few minutes later I was sorry.
What harm is there to accept his prayer? I could borrow
his God for a while.

MRS. ABERNATHY

Doctor:

Soft trees against blue sky. That is how
Mrs. Abernathy described it
before she died. A small barn bent further
than my arthritic spine. A white clapboard house,
a wood-burning stove, and a bathtub
so big you could swim to China.

The autopsy report said pneumonia.
It might have included the thousand little bone holes
from the breast cancer that began five years earlier.
It might have reported how her skin peeled away
like birch bark or that her mitral valve clicked shut
like a rusted door.

NAMES

Patient:

Angela, would you see if there's any free space
on the wall for this wonderful card? It's hard to believe
a five-year-old can draw like this. She's so precious,
and look here, it's signed Arielle. Isn't it lovely?
Names are so much more interesting today, like Letisha,
Rima, and Ice Tea. My older brother Harry
is named after an uncle who died in World War II.
My parents narrowed down mine to months: April, May,
and June. Come to think of it, it's awfully ironic being hospitalized
these three weeks. Is there some confluence in our lives
with our name? Are we marked from the start?
Might things be different had they chosen Cassandra,
Sun Blossom, Starship Enterprise, or Hope?

NOT GOD

Doctor:

I thought to delay the answer, camouflage
it, by waiting until he asked another
question. But he prefaced the question with,

I know you're not God. This is commonly said
to me, second in frequency only to, What
would you do if it was your father, or wife,

et cetera? I accept this statement of my undeity
to be rhetorical, a mechanism to permit me
to be imprecise, to use phrases like *it depends*

upon many factors and *a range of.* But lately
I'm increasingly tempted to say, How do you know
I'm not God? What gives you such certainty?

Do you say this to your lawyer, accountant,
or mother-in-law? And if I'm not God, then why
ask me a question that only God can answer?

FOUR WEEKS

Patient:

Let me tell you what the Angel of Death
looks like: five feet two, elderly, slightly obese,
hair dyed gunmetal black. I know this because

Mrs. Abeloff, in 1128, and Mr. Jamison,
in 1136, "succumbed peacefully last night."
What they have in common is cancer

and Mrs. Hendricks on the night shift. She's
the little secret no one talks about. It's simple.
She comes in, checks the pulse, presses

the morphine pump, and waits. That's it. She has
a three A.M. snack, signs out at seven, and goes home.

WHAT'D I SAY

Doctor:

Mr. Beringer had iridium seeds implanted in his prostate.
Mrs. Alawaudy is receiving infusional 5-FU through
a silicon stent threaded into her hepatic artery. And Jane Holloway

has a titanium plate replacing a portion of her pelvis
riddled with metastases. Here one quickly assimilates
this language of hisses and clicks, where

every Chubby Checker and Ray Charles song
that I had so loved now sounds thin and trite, little monosyllabic
coughs against the hurricane of carcinomatosis.

GUIDE WIRE

Patient:

I see a Metro-North train is delayed more than three hours. Apparently a man tried to jump from the window and was subdued by a quick-acting Samaritan. Today something similar occurred while I was waiting in radiology. A woman weighing more than three hundred pounds got stuck inside the MRI. I could hear her screaming frantically. Someone reached in with a syringe and injected her with Valium, which had no effect. I tell you it was completely hopeless until this young technician ingeniously saved the day. He doused long lengths of gauze in petroleum jelly, then using a guide wire fished them around her. They said she slipped out easily, squealing all the while like a big greased pig, as everyone applauded. I hope that young man goes into medicine. God knows they need people with a little inventiveness and a good pair of hands. The head cardiologist couldn't thread a catheter into the coronary artery in three patients this morning. It isn't a secret. I am inundated with statistics. They soak me as I wait in the hallways.

CHAIR

Patient:

Pale anemic plastic chair pitted by years
of metal keys protruding from back pockets.
I pass it twenty-eight times on my half-mile
morning perambulation of the treatment unit.
Today I detoured through detox. (The door
was left open.) The decor is different: bright
floral wallpaper, Danish teak furniture, and
a nursing station that you would walk up to
and ask a question. A young man
in a light blue cotton gown open in back
was lugging an IV pole. He was nervously talking
with an unlit cigarette between his thin yellow fingers.
His forearm was covered with deep gray potholes
and long purple spidery lines. The IV tubing entered
near his neck. He's out of veins, Josey
later explained.

ALCHEMY

Doctor:

Stone turns to buttermilk, pipe
cleaners to dreams, necromancers
and pythons to aristocrats
and ballerinas. Here platinum

shrinks lung cancer. Taxol,
from tree bark, withers
an ovarian metastasis into nothingness,
and prednisone cures lymphoma.

What is this, then, if not alchemy,
potions and witches' brews,
toxins turned to gold, barbed wire
into silvery South Sea pearls?

SIGN!

Patient:

What do I want? A dish of ice cream (chocolate)
with no nurse or relative admonishing me. I want to stroll outside
at noon (it's against the rules), but I'd have to sign out
against medical advice. And I want to refuse to sign
the surgery consent—no, I don't want another central line
or a D.N.R. Damned if they want you to die
at three A.M., run in, pound your chest fifteen minutes,
put those paddles on, hit the switch, and insert an airway for a
    ventilator.
No, sir. They don't want you drooling and defecating in bed.
Just sign the consent, and if you might not be so inclined,
they can always convince a relative (there's a clause that asserts
you're not competent). I know. I signed a D.N.R. for my father.
They put it in front of you, and God knows you don't want
to cause a loved one more harm, you don't want to become
a frigging nuisance. So you sign it. That's right, sweetie,
you sign on the dotted line.

GRANDMA KATY

Doctor:

The sky a July coconut haze,
the blue and white enamel signs:
50TH ST. and 14TH AVE.

The two-family brick house, one in
from the northeast corner,
is a small religious school now.

Its concrete stoop, four steps
(I had guessed six), is painted over
yellow too many times, and the chipped

balustrade to the left,
against which I fell, is sanded smooth.
My memory is frozen into still frames.

In one, I am on the top step
seated on my new blue bicycle. In another,
my grandmother wraps a cold rag

around my forearm. A pea green housedress
with small white flowers billows like a tent.
Steam lifts off the clear soup filling

a broad maroon bowl. A thin stick of celery.
Two carrot chips. A chicken foot
with puckered skin and three large toes.

WOUND

Patient:

My grandmother used to say
my imagination was unhealthy.
(I think of her a lot lately.)

I had set up intricate games,
and my rules required that
each participant choose a piece

and tell the story of its journey
from beginning to end. Mine
might take two hours.

My protagonist sometimes lived
a simple life and always died
at the end. Angela comes in

to change the dressing.
She says it is healing nicely.
Outside a jet streams by. It is

as distant as a straw blown
from a crystal glass at breakfast
on a small skiff near the equator.

LECTURE TO THIRD-YEAR MEDICAL STUDENTS

Doctor:

My first recommendation: Suction an ample
volume of bone marrow, separate a sample

for pathology, incubate the rest in fetal
media, freeze it, administer a lethal

dose of chemo, and then reinfuse
the marrow as soon as the white count is reduced

below one thousand. If the extracted marrow
is first allowed

to incubate with several newer monoclonal antibodies,
residual cancer cells are killed and metastases

are less likely. A frequent
problem in these young patients

is the development of resistance,
which is related to the presence

of the c-Ras gene, even
when

treatments have initially
been effective, especially

in highly aggressive lymphomas such as this.
There's very little chance that his

tumor will respond to such drastic treatment,
and indeed the mortality from marrow replacement

exceeds the cure rate. However, in my opinion,
there's no other option.

STRAWS

Patient:

They feed me everything
through a straw. First time I can recall
using one I was three. It was the summer
my parents rented a bungalow in Rockaway,
B. 49TH ST. Uncle Isadore and Aunt Dora
were closer to the beach.

Every morning after breakfast of toast
and oatmeal I'd sneak in the back door
of the Hellers', and Mrs. Rosen,
the grandmother with a large black mole
next to her left nostril, would feed me
pancakes, syrup, home fries, and

a vanilla milk shake with a plain paper straw.
Later they came with accordion folds,
then plastic and designer straws:
looped and multicolored. Now it is paper
again, and the nurse speaks to me
as if I were three.

LIKE ME

Doctor:

When I was two, my doctor
had a large house
on Cortelyou Road. The exam room
smelled like a dead frog
and my temperature was taken
rectally. By age five
I was injected with tetracycline
monthly
by Dr. Ryan. He later died

of lung cancer. Who influenced me
the most, a medical school
interviewer asked. Thirty years later
I still don't know. Today
a sixteen-year-old girl said
she'd like to be
just like me as I pushed
her third course
of chemotherapy.

REWARD

Patient:

I used to think that way,
to believe there was reward
for good deeds. Yet even
as a youngster I was warned
the rewards weren't obvious
or were deferred to the hereafter.

Some people never wonder
what they'll say when told
the end is near. They don't say,
Why me? When told they've
a few years left they're consoled.
I prefer not knowing. It sufficed

to know everyone died sooner or later.
The *later* was consolation.
If you say this disease was there
for years, that's no consolation
since now I know and
knowing's no reward.

BRINE

Doctor:

I am swimming across a large pool of brine,
clawing my way through dense algae,
and just at the other end several adults are cheering
me on. You can make it, they say. One little girl

watches me. She is five, wearing
a yellow tulle dress and yellow ballerina slippers.
She says nothing. She never speaks, no matter
how many times I swim toward her.

I tire more easily now. I have been doing this
over fifteen years, and I've watched them, hundreds
of them, when I fail, and even when I succeed,
it has become less and less solace for the next effort.

It is like this being an oncologist, and each time
I enter the brine I try to be buoyant. I try
to concentrate on the other side but the light
glares blindingly off that little girl in yellow.

ROOM 1122

Patient:

Soldiers march outside my room all night.
They began when Mrs. Carson moved in,
a little old lady half covered in saran wrap.
It was late Wednesday or Thursday. No matter.
There is nothing I can do; she is on a ventilator
that bleeps like a parakeet, and Angela insists
the reason I can't sleep is that I nap too much
during the day. Even if it's true, whose fault is it,
with six soldiers and two janitors banging behind
with mops and pails? I could ask to move
from 1122, but it will be a great nuisance
to remove all the cards on the wall, and at least here
I am near the nursing station just in case
this minipump stops working again. The intern
explained it's interactive. I push this button
whenever I wish. *Wish* is the wrong verb,
young man, I point out. Do I wait until the pain
reaches my epiglottis, or do I give another shove
of the button and feel my lips thicken like oatmeal,
my bowels stiffen like an old rubber tire tube,
and my brain unwind like a spool of yarn
my cat bats across the kitchen floor?

CANCER PRAYER

Doctor:

Tell me, please, how to be cavalier
after twenty years of treating patients
with arrogant adjectives, with verbs
too powerful to be comprehensible,
and nouns with such innocent sounds—
*lymphoma, melanoma, breast
cancer*—that they shatter my ears.

Hope is sometimes a puddle
of stale rainwater for a parched mouth,
though I must continue to pray.

I pray that the power that makes genetic strands
proliferate aberrantly allows us to reverse it,
to discover a gene insertion to correct
each untoward event, and if not, then just today,
I pray that the little boy with Wilm's tumor
will have no side effects from his chemotherapy,
that this one woman with ovary cancer

in room 1122 will have a complete remission.
The word *cure,* dear God, is always
near my lips, though I have been constrained from
saying it aloud. Allow me at least to think it.

66

HOME

Patient:

I miss the leaves coming in
    on the old maple. My bones
bend against themselves.
    As if dignity doesn't matter.

As if I can be sustained by
    Bonnie's hand. She curls up
next to me and rubs
    my belly. My skin folds

like cellophane. I am molecules
    breaking apart. I cry just to change
my linens again. The distance
    narrows in my veins.

THE BRIDGE 2

Patient:

I was never good at volleyball. I can't
sail. I've never been to Bangkok or Peru.
I've published twenty-two papers on early
adolescence. Mostly theoretical. Like measuring
intellect. Like imagining a bridge that can cross
the Atlantic. Like imagining sound
without my children.

My daddy whispers algebraic equations
to me, ancient paradigms, he says,
taught to him in heaven by Copernicus.
What is its purpose? I ask. To understand
monumentality, he responds.
The bridge has seven layers of titanium cable
bound together by intention

and rooted in recitations. Seventeen
wise men safeguard the structure.
God meditates in the middle tower while
the eighteenth sings lullabies.

WHAT I AM

Doctor:

You ask me how I know.
    It's hard to say. It's not
something I could easily
    teach, like palpation
of an enlarged liver.

I couldn't describe it
    with precision, e.g.,
sixth-nerve palsy, the sound
    of mitral stenosis. Still,
after twenty years,

it's unmistakable. A fine tremor
    of his eyebrow,
the skin below his chin
    like papier-mâché,
the way his shoulder

tilts back to the right.
    He has less than
a few months to live. I can't say
    it's vascular,
or neurologic, or even

cancer, which I see
    every day. I only know
it's progressive
    and irreversible. It's
what I am proficient at.

Pale anemic plastic chair, pitted by years
of metal keys protruding from back pockets.
I pass it twenty eight times on my half-mile
morning perambulation of the treatment unit.

About the Playwright

Marc J. Straus is a practicing oncologist and the recipient of the Robert Penn Warren Award in the Humanities from Yale University Medical School. He is the author of *One Word* and *Symmetry,* both published by TriQuarterly Books/Northwestern University Press, and his poems have appeared in many journals, including *Kenyon Review, Ploughshares,* and *Tikkun.* He lives in Chappaqua, New York.